Level F • Book 1

QuickReads®
A Research-Based Fluency Program

Elfrieda H. Hiebert, Ph.D.

MODERN CURRICULUM PRESS
Pearson Learning Group

Program Reviewers and Consultants

Dr. Barbara A. Baird
Director of Federal Programs/Richardson ISD
Richardson, TX

Dr. Kate Kinsella
Dept. of Secondary Education and Step to College Program
San Francisco State University
San Francisco, CA

Pat Sears
Early Child Coordinator/Virginia Beach Public Schools
Virginia Beach, VA

Dr. Judith B. Smith
Supervisor of ESOL and World and Classical Languages/Baltimore City Public Schools
Baltimore, MD

The following people have contributed to the development of this program:

Art and Design: Kathleen Ellison, Denise Ingrassia, Salita Mehta,
  Dan Thomas, Dan Trush

Editorial: Lynn W. Kloss

Marketing: Alison Bruno

Production/Manufacturing: Louis Campos, Michele Uhl

Publishing Operations: Jennifer Van Der Heide

ISBN 0-7652-7206-7

Printed in the United States of America

2 3 4 5 6 7 8 9 10   09 08 07 06

1-800-321-3106
www.pearsonlearning.com

Contents

SOCIAL STUDIES

Speeches That Inspire

The Power of Speech 10

The Gettysburg Address 12

A Day of Infamy 14

A Call to Service 16

I Have a Dream 18

Speeches That Inspire Review 20

 Connect Your Ideas 23

Contents

SOCIAL STUDIES

American Pioneers

John Muir 24

Eleanor Roosevelt 26

The Little Rock Nine 28

Neil Armstrong 30

David Ho 32

American Pioneers Review 34

 Connect Your Ideas 37

4

SOCIAL
STUDIES

Celebrating Independence

Canada Day 38

Mexican Independence Day 40

Independence Day in the Philippines 42

Freedom Day 44

Bastille Day 46

Celebrating Independence Review 48

 Connect Your Ideas 51

Contents

SCIENCE **Cells**

The Smallest Units of Life 52

Trillions of Cells 54

Making New Cells 56

One-Celled Living Things 58

Cells and Human Disease 60

Cells Review 62

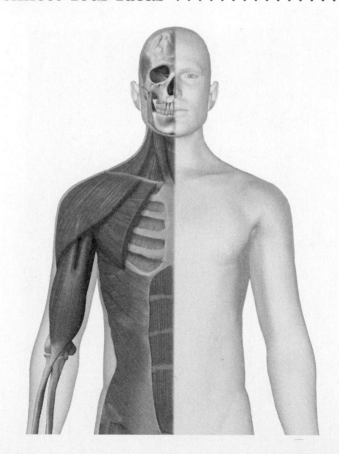 Connect Your Ideas 65

SCIENCE **The Human Nervous System**

What Does the Nervous System Do? 66

The Parts of the Nervous System 68

The Control Center 70

Sending Messages 72

The Super-Highway 74

The Human Nervous System Review 76

Connect Your Ideas 79

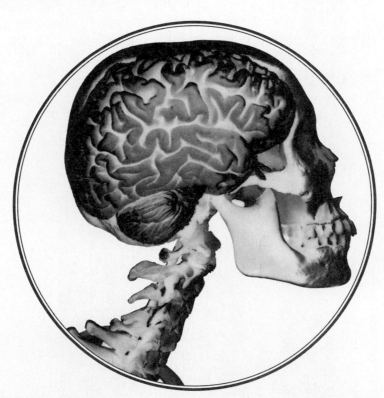

Contents

SCIENCE **Symbiosis**

What Is Symbiosis? 80

Mutual Benefits 82

Benefits and Costs 84

Benefits for One 86

Symbiosis in Ants 88

Symbiosis Review 90

 Connect Your Ideas 93

Reading Log 94

Self-Check Graph 96

Acknowledgments

All photography © Pearson Education Inc. (PEI) unless otherwise specifically noted.

Cover: Tom Boyle/Getty Images, Inc. 3: © Bob Adelman/Magnum Photos. 4: © Bettmann/Corbis. 5: AP/Wide World Photo. 7: David Barlow/AFP/Getty Images, Inc. 8: © Sea Images, Inc./Animals Animals/Earth Scenes. 10: © Robert Brenner/PhotoEdit. 12: Reza Estakhrian/Stone Allstock/Getty Images, Inc. 14: *t.* The Granger Collection; *b.* © Bettmann/Corbis. 16: AP/Wide World Photo. 18: © Bob Adelman/Magnum Photos. 24: *t.* Jeff Foott/PictureQuest; *b.* © Corbis. 26: AP/Wide World Photo. 28: © Bettmann/Corbis. 30: *t.* NASA/Photo Researchers, Inc.; *b.* © Bettmann/Corbis. 32: © Hashimoto Noboru/Corbis. 38: © Garry Black/Masterfile. 40: Jorge Silva/AFP/ Getty Images, Inc. 42: AP/Wide World Photo. 44: AP/Wide World Photo. 46: AP/Wide World Photo. 52: *l.* Omikron/Photo Researchers, Inc.; *r.* Science & Society Picture Library. 56: Joubert/Photo Researchers, Inc. 58: Photo Researchers, Inc. 60: © Jim Dowdalls/Photo Researchers, Inc. 66: © Royalty-Free/Corbis. 70: David Barlow/AFP/ Getty Images, Inc. 72: Alfred Pasieka/Photo Researchers, Inc. 74: © Photopress Ampas/Corbis. 80: Norbert Wu/Minden Pictures. 82: © Sea Images, Inc./Animals Animals/Earth Scenes. 84: John Watkins/FLPA/Minden Pictures. 86: © William Manning/Corbis. 88: © OSF/David Thompson/Animals Animals/Earth Scenes.

Speeches That Inspire

Speakers can give people information or inspire them to take action.

The Power of Speech

Speakers can affect people deeply. The words in a speech can calm, anger, or inspire the people in an audience. However,[25] the way in which the words are said can also affect people.

Today, speeches can be recorded on audiotapes and videotapes. People who were not[50] in the audience when the speech was delivered can hear and see the event. They can be calmed, angered, or inspired, just as the first[75] audience was.

A written copy of a speech can affect people, too. Many famous speeches were made before audiotapes and videotapes were invented. Patrick Henry[100] made a famous speech that ended with the words "Give me liberty or give me death." Even today, the words that Patrick Henry spoke in 1775 inspire Americans to fight for their liberty.[133]

Speeches That Inspire

In the Lincoln Memorial in Washington, D.C., the words of the Gettysburg Address are carved into the wall behind President Lincoln.

The Gettysburg Address

Of the many battles that were fought between the Union and Confederate armies during the U.S. Civil War, one of the worst[25] was fought near Gettysburg, Pennsylvania. Thousands of Union and Confederate soldiers died in the Battle of Gettysburg. To honor the dead, the people of Gettysburg[50] began making a cemetery.

At the service for the National Cemetery in 1863, one speaker spoke for two hours. However, it is the speech of[75] President Lincoln, who spoke for only a few minutes, that is remembered. President Lincoln said that the best way to honor the fallen soldiers was[100] to finish the task of reuniting the country. By doing this, he said that "government of the people, by the people, for the people, shall not perish from the earth."[130]

Speeches That Inspire

President Franklin Roosevelt speaks to Congress about Japan's attack on Pearl Harbor.

A Day of Infamy

On December 7, 1941, Pearl Harbor, in Hawaii, was attacked by Japan. The surprise attack killed many people and destroyed many [25] ships. People feared that the United States mainland would be attacked, just like Hawaii had been.

The day after the Pearl Harbor attack, President Franklin [50] Roosevelt spoke to Congress, describing December 7 as "a date which will live in infamy." He said that Americans "will not only defend ourselves . . . but [75] will make very certain that this . . . shall never endanger us again."

President Roosevelt said that Americans must work together to prevent future attacks. The speech [100] lessened people's fears. It also inspired them to action. Throughout the war that followed, people remembered President Roosevelt's "Day of Infamy" speech as a reminder to work together to win the war. [132]

Speeches That Inspire

President John F. Kennedy is shown giving his inaugural address. In his speech, President Kennedy inspired people to work for others.

A Call to Service

American presidents begin a new term by giving a speech called an inaugural address. In 1961, when John F. Kennedy became[25] president, four countries had nuclear bombs, and many people were afraid of the damage nuclear bombs could cause.

In his inaugural address, President Kennedy asked[50] people to work on their shared problems, not their differences. He challenged Americans to "ask not what your country can do for you—ask what[75] you can do for your country." President Kennedy also challenged people around the world to "ask not what America will do for you, but what[100] together we can do for the freedom of man."

President Kennedy's inaugural address inspired people to work for freedom and human rights. It said that working together would make people safe—and free.[133]

Speeches That Inspire

Dr. Martin Luther King, Jr., inspired people to have dreams
and to work to achieve them.

I Have a Dream

On a hot day in 1963, more than 250,000 people gathered at the Lincoln Memorial in Washington, D.C., to hear Dr.[25] Martin Luther King, Jr., speak. Standing in front of the Lincoln Memorial, Dr. King said that he wanted equal rights for all people. Dr. King[50] reminded people that African Americans did not have the same rights as white Americans did.

Dr. King repeated the phrase "I have a dream" to[75] describe his hopes for the future, including his "dream that my four children will one day live in a nation where they will not be[100] judged by the color of their skin, but by the content of their character." Dr. King's "I Have a Dream" speech continues to inspire people to dream—and to work—for human rights.[133]

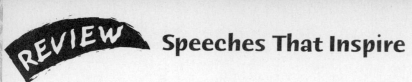

Speeches That Inspire

Write words that will help you remember what you learned.

The Power of Speech

_____

_____

_____

_____

The Gettysburg Address

_____

_____

_____

_____

A Day of Infamy

_____

_____

_____

_____

A Call to Service

_____

_____

_____

_____

I Have a Dream

_____

_____

_____

_____

The Power of Speech

1. Another good name for "The Power of Speech" is ___

   Ⓐ "Give Me Liberty."

   Ⓑ "How Speeches Affect People."

   Ⓒ "Recorded Speeches."

   Ⓓ "Famous Speeches."

2. Why are some speeches powerful?

   _____

   _____

   _____

The Gettysburg Address

1. What is the Gettysburg Address?

   Ⓐ a famous Civil War battle

   Ⓑ where President Lincoln lived

   Ⓒ a speech President Lincoln gave

   Ⓓ a cemetery for Civil War veterans

2. What was President Lincoln's message in the Gettysburg Address?

   _____

   _____

   _____

A Day of Infamy

1. "A Day of Infamy" is MAINLY about ___

   Ⓐ what happened in World War II.

   Ⓑ why President Roosevelt wrote speeches.

   Ⓒ why Japan attacked Pearl Harbor.

   Ⓓ President Roosevelt's speech after the Pearl Harbor attack.

2. How did people respond to President Roosevelt's speech?

   _____

   _____

   _____

A Call to Service

1. An inaugural address is a speech that ___

   Ⓐ tells about how people should fight a war.

   Ⓑ American presidents give at the start of a term.

   Ⓒ tells people why they should vote for someone.

   Ⓓ American presidents give when they leave office.

2. What did President Kennedy say in his inaugural address?

   _____

   _____

   _____

I Have a Dream

1. What was the main idea of Dr. King's speech?

   Ⓐ that everyone should be able to dream

   Ⓑ that all people should have equal rights

   Ⓒ that Dr. King dreamed of being president

   Ⓓ that people gathered to hear Dr. King speak

2. What was Dr. King's dream?

   _____

   _____

   _____

Connect Your Ideas

1. How did two of the speeches in this topic inspire people?

   _____

   _____

   _____

2. Why do you think the speakers in this topic wanted to give speeches that inspired people?

   _____

   _____

   _____

American Pioneers

John Muir worked to preserve wilderness areas around the United States.

John Muir

John Muir was a pioneer in preserving, or protecting, places of natural beauty in the United States. One hundred years ago, most Americans[25] had not thought about the need to preserve such places.

John Muir spread the message of land preservation in several ways. He took long walking[50] trips through wilderness areas, often by himself. On one trip, he walked 1,000 miles from the middle of the United States to the Gulf of[75] Mexico.

In articles and books, John Muir wrote about the wildflowers, trees, insects, and birds that he saw in the wilderness. He also gave speeches[100] about his travels and about the need to preserve places of natural beauty. John Muir made people think about why the wilderness is important and why people should work to save it.[132]

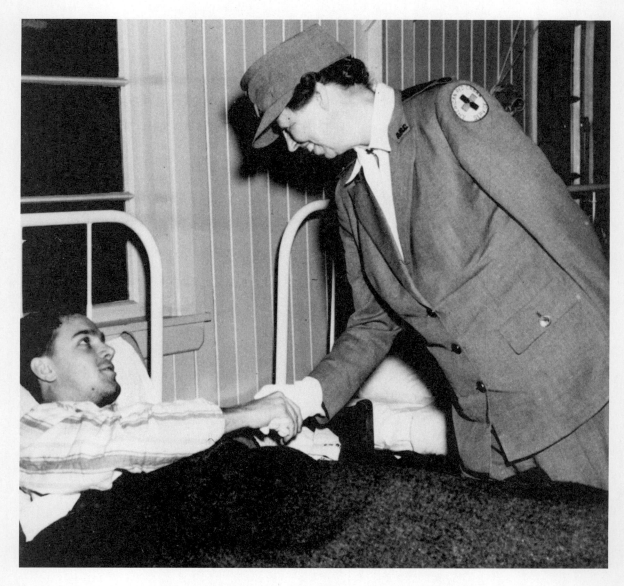

Eleanor Roosevelt visited people in hospitals, schools, and many other places to find out how the government could help them.

Eleanor Roosevelt

Eleanor Roosevelt was a pioneer in the human-rights movement. She was also the wife of Franklin Roosevelt, the 32nd president of the[25] United States.

Before becoming president, Franklin Roosevelt had a disease that weakened his legs. When President Roosevelt couldn't travel, Eleanor Roosevelt traveled for him. She[50] visited hospitals, schools, and factories in the United States and around the world. Then, she reported on these visits to the president. She also spoke[75] and wrote about improving living conditions for all Americans and about equal rights for women.

After President Roosevelt died, Eleanor Roosevelt became a special delegate[100] to the United Nations. As a delegate, Eleanor Roosevelt led the writing of a declaration of human rights. This declaration stated that all humans have rights, a new idea in many countries.[132]

Many white people did not want the Little Rock Nine
to go to an all-white school in Arkansas.

The Little Rock Nine

In 1954, the U.S. Supreme Court declared that separate schools for African Americans and whites were against the law. However, in[25] 1957, 17 states still had separate schools for African American and white students. That year, nine African American students enrolled in an all-white high[50] school in Little Rock, Arkansas.

The Little Rock Nine, as they were called, were the first African American students to enroll in the Arkansas school.[75] Soldiers had to protect the Little Rock Nine from people who tried to prevent the students from going to school.

Despite these hardships, the Little[100] Rock Nine kept going to school. Finally, African American students were accepted in all-white schools. The Little Rock Nine had helped all American children gain the right to an equal education.[132]

American Pioneers

Shown here are the three astronauts from *Apollo 11*—Neil Armstrong (left), Buzz Aldrin (center), and Michael Collins (right)—and Armstrong's footprint on the Moon.

Neil Armstrong

On May 25, 1961, President Kennedy said, "This nation should commit itself to achieving the goal, before this decade is out, of landing [25] a man on the Moon and returning him safely to Earth." American scientists worked hard inventing and testing spacecraft. Then, on July 20, 1969, the [50] U.S. spacecraft *Apollo 11* landed on the Moon.

Astronaut Neil Armstrong was the first person to step onto the Moon. As he did, Armstrong said, [75] "That's one small step for man, one giant leap for mankind." Another Apollo astronaut, Buzz Aldrin, followed Armstrong onto the Moon.

Armstrong and Aldrin collected [100] soil and rocks on the Moon. Then, four days later, the *Apollo 11* spacecraft and its crew returned safely to Earth. President Kennedy's goal had been achieved before the decade was over. [132]

Dr. David Ho's experiments are helping people who have HIV, including basketball star Magic Johnson.

David Ho

In 1981, doctors identified a new illness caused by the human immunodeficiency virus, or HIV. This virus makes the immune system deficient, or [25] weak. Because their immune system protects people from disease, having a deficient immune system means that a person can get sick easily.

David Ho was [50] a pioneer in learning how HIV attacks the immune system. Dr. Ho's experiments showed that the virus attacks the immune system as soon as it [75] enters the body. Before Dr. Ho made this discovery, doctors treated people only when they already had a disease. Dr. Ho's experiments showed that HIV [100] must be stopped *before* it made people sick.

There is still no cure for the human immunodeficiency virus. However, David Ho and others continue to search for ways to protect people against it. [133]

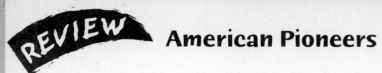

REVIEW American Pioneers

Write words that will help you remember what you learned.

John Muir

_____

_____

_____

_____

Eleanor Roosevelt

_____

_____

_____

_____

The Little Rock Nine

_____

_____

_____

_____

Neil Armstrong

_____

_____

_____

_____

David Ho

_____

_____

_____

_____

John Muir

1. Why was John Muir an American pioneer?

   Ⓐ He told people that they should travel in the wilderness.

   Ⓑ He discovered new trees, birds, and insects in wild areas.

   Ⓒ He helped people understand why they should preserve the wilderness.

   Ⓓ He was the first person to walk to the Gulf of Mexico.

2. How did John Muir help people understand his ideas?

   _____

   _____

   _____

Eleanor Roosevelt

1. Eleanor Roosevelt was an American pioneer because ___

   Ⓐ she worked for human rights.

   Ⓑ she was the wife of President Franklin Roosevelt.

   Ⓒ she gave speeches at the United Nations.

   Ⓓ she traveled for President Roosevelt.

2. How did Eleanor Roosevelt help other people?

   _____

   _____

   _____

The Little Rock Nine

1. Who were the Little Rock Nine?

   Ⓐ soldiers who helped African American students

   Ⓑ African American students in Arkansas

   Ⓒ judges on the U.S. Supreme Court

   Ⓓ laws that allowed students to have an equal education

2. Why were the Little Rock Nine American pioneers?

   _____

   _____

   _____

Neil Armstrong

1. Why was Neil Armstrong an American pioneer?

   Ⓐ He helped American scientists understand soil on Earth.

   Ⓑ He told President Kennedy that people should go to the Moon.

   Ⓒ He helped American scientists invent spacecraft.

   Ⓓ He was the first man to walk on the Moon.

2. What did Neil Armstrong mean when he said, "That's one small step for man, one giant leap for mankind"?

   _____

   _____

   _____

David Ho

1. David Ho is an American pioneer because he discovered ___

   Ⓐ that a new disease was caused by HIV.

   Ⓑ that there is a cure for HIV.

   Ⓒ how HIV attacks the immune system.

   Ⓓ how the immune system works.

2. What did David Ho discover about HIV?

   _____

   _____

Connect Your Ideas

1. What is a pioneer?

   _____

   _____

   _____

2. Describe two qualities that a person needs to become a pioneer.

   _____

   _____

   _____

Celebrating Independence

The Canadian people celebrate their independence from
Great Britain on July 1.

Canada Day

On July 4th, the people of the United States celebrate their independence with parades and fireworks. On July 1st, the people of Canada[25] celebrate their own independence with parades and fireworks. On this day, called Canada Day, Canadians celebrate the day their national government was established.

Like the[50] United States, Canada began as a group of British colonies. Unlike the United States, however, Canada did not have a war to gain its independence[75] from Great Britain.

Instead, on July 1, 1867, the British North America Act gave the Canadian colonies the right to form their own national government.[100] Canada was the first country to gain its independence from Great Britain in this way. Since then, more than 50 other former colonies have gained their independence from Great Britain in a similar way.[134]

Celebrating Independence

In Mexico City, the people celebrate their independence with fireworks.

Mexican Independence Day

Mexico's national celebration marks the beginning of its war for independence. During the night of September 16, 1810, Father Hidalgo rang the [25] church bell in the village of Dolores. When the people of Dolores gathered in the plaza, Father Hidalgo read a proclamation of independence that he [50] and others had written. The proclamation ended with these words: "Mexicans, long live Mexico!" This call began Mexico's war of independence against Spain. The war [75] lasted until 1821.

To celebrate their independence, Mexicans gather in plazas on the night of September 16th to hear the cry, "Mexicans, long live Mexico!" [100] In Mexico City, the Mexican president gives this cry and rings the bell that Father Hidalgo rang in Dolores. People then spend the next day celebrating their independence with parades and fireworks. [132]

Celebrating Independence

The people of the Philippine Islands
celebrate their independence by raising their flag.

Independence Day in the Philippines

On June 12, 1898, the Spanish, who had ruled the Philippine Islands for hundreds of years, were defeated in a [25] war. The country that had won the war—the United States—then took over governing the Philippines.

For almost 50 years, the United States guided [50] the government of the Philippines. However, on July 4, 1946, the Philippine Islands became an independent nation.

Although the Philippine Islands gained its independence from [75] the United States on July 4th, the people of the Philippines decided to celebrate their independence on June 12th. That is because the national flag [100] of the Philippine Islands was first flown on June 12, 1898. This is the day that the people of the Philippines mark as the day when their country's independence really began. [131]

Celebrating Independence

On Freedom Day, people in South Africa celebrate their independence with parades and dances.

Freedom Day

In most countries, the national holiday celebrates the country's independence from the rule of another nation. Until recently, South Africa had a national[25] holiday of this kind. This holiday recognized South Africa's independence from Great Britain, which it gained in 1961.

The independence from Great Britain, however, did[50] not mean that all South Africans were free. The laws of South Africa favored white people. Black people had few rights, could live only in[75] certain places, and could not vote in national elections. Finally, on April 27, 1994, South Africa held its first national election in which all people[100] could vote.

South Africans now celebrate April 27th as their national holiday, not the day their country became independent of Great Britain. Freedom Day celebrates the day all South Africans gained their rights.[133]

Celebrating Independence

The French people celebrate their independence on Bastille Day
with fireworks and parades.

Bastille Day

By 1789, many French citizens had become unhappy with their monarch, Louis XVI. France had been a monarchy, or a government ruled by[25] a king, for several hundred years. However, the people wanted to replace their monarchy with a government that would be fair to all citizens.

King[50] Louis XVI had put citizens who disagreed with him into a prison called the Bastille. For many French citizens, the Bastille was a symbol of[75] what was wrong with France.

On July 14, 1789, an angry mob stormed the Bastille and freed its prisoners. Soon after, the people overthrew the[100] monarchy and established a form of government called a republic. The republic gave French citizens their rights. Today, the French celebrate July 14th, Bastille Day, as the day their republic was born.[132]

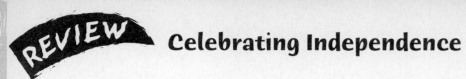

Celebrating Independence

Write words that will help you remember what you learned.

Canada Day

_____
_____
_____
_____

Mexican Independence Day

_____
_____
_____
_____

Independence Day in the Philippines

_____
_____
_____
_____

Freedom Day

_____
_____
_____

Bastille Day

_____
_____
_____
_____

Canada Day

1. What form of government did Canada have before it became independent?

   Ⓐ It was a colony in Europe.

   Ⓑ It was a British colony.

   Ⓒ It was part of the United States.

   Ⓓ It was a state in North America.

2. Compare how Canada and the United States gained their independence.

   _____

   _____

   _____

Mexican Independence Day

1. From what country did Mexico gain its independence?

   Ⓐ England

   Ⓑ Dolores

   Ⓒ the United States

   Ⓓ Spain

2. How did Father Hidalgo help Mexico gain its independence?

   _____

   _____

   _____

Celebrating Independence

Independence Day in the Philippines

1. What two countries ruled the Philippines before it became independent?

    Ⓐ Mexico and Spain

    Ⓑ the United Nations and Europe

    Ⓒ Spain and the United States

    Ⓓ the United States and Europe

2. Why do you think the people of the Philippines celebrate the day their flag was first flown?

    _____

    _____

    _____

Freedom Day

1. Another good name for "Freedom Day" is ___

    Ⓐ "Celebrating Independence From Great Britain."

    Ⓑ "A Change in South Africa's Laws."

    Ⓒ "Elections for South Africa."

    Ⓓ "Celebrating Rights for All South Africans."

2. Why did South Africa change its day of independence?

    _____

    _____

    _____

Bastille Day

1. The French people wanted a government ___

   Ⓐ that was ruled by a king.

   Ⓑ that would be fair to everyone.

   Ⓒ that would storm the Bastille.

   Ⓓ that was ruled by a monarchy.

2. Why did the French people storm the Bastille?

   _____

   _____

   _____

Connect Your Ideas

1. What is one reason all of these countries celebrate their independence?

   _____

   _____

   _____

2. Why do you think a country might want its independence from another country?

   _____

   _____

   _____

Cells

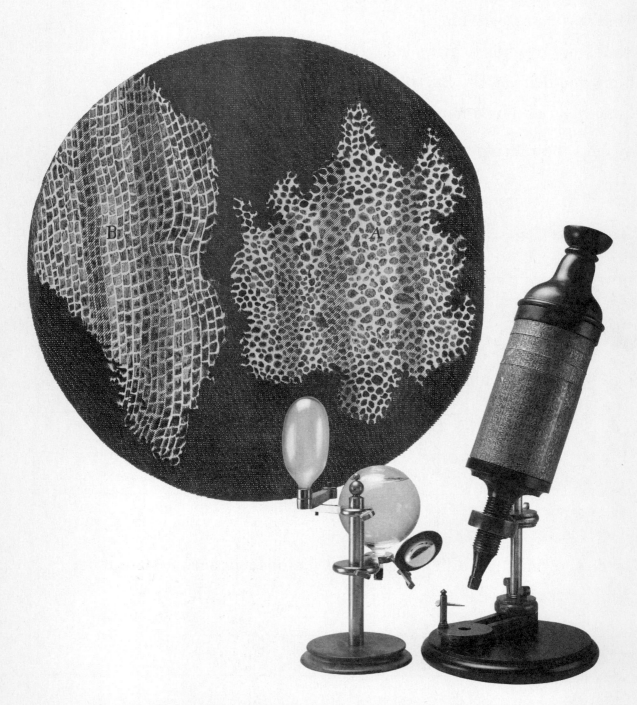

Robert Hooke's microscope is shown next to drawings of two kinds of cork cells.

The Smallest Units of Life

When scientist Robert Hooke looked through his microscope at a piece of cork, he saw what looked like little rooms.[25] Hooke called these shapes *cells*, after the Latin word *cella*, which means "room." Cells, which are so small that they can only be seen through[50] a microscope, are the smallest units of living material. Hooke was the first person to identify them.

Although both plants and animals have cells, their[75] cells differ in some ways. Unlike animal cells, plant cells have strong walls. Because plants do not have bones, cell walls help plants stand up.[100] Plant cells also have substances called chloroplasts. Chloroplasts use sunlight to make food for the plant. Animal cells do not have chloroplasts, so animals cannot make food. Instead, they must find it.[132]

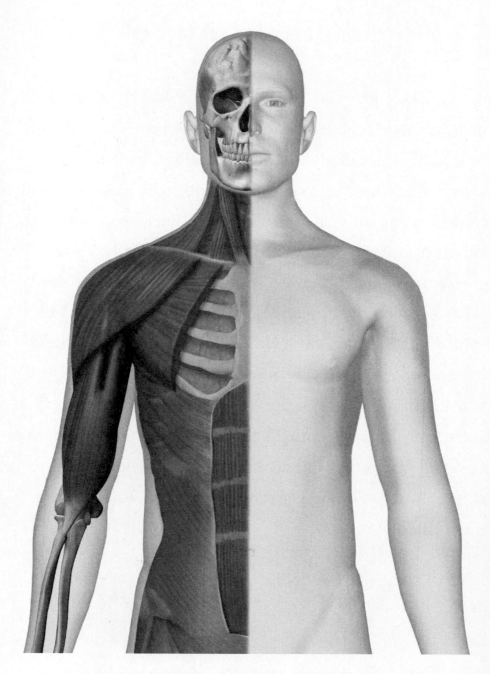

The left side of this drawing shows some of the muscles, bones, and organs in the human body.

Trillions of Cells

A human body has more than 75 trillion cells. These 75 trillion cells combine to form the body's systems. Thousands of cells[25] also join to form tissues, such as bone or skin. Tissues then join to form organs, such as the lungs or the heart. Finally, tissues[50] and organs form systems that perform major jobs, such as breathing.

One example of a human system is the respiratory system. In the respiratory system,[75] the cells of the lungs, heart, breathing muscles, and air passages work together to move air in and out of the body.

The respiratory system[100] also works with the other human systems to digest food, send messages to and from the brain, and perform other tasks. All 75 trillion cells work together to keep a human body alive.[133]

Cells

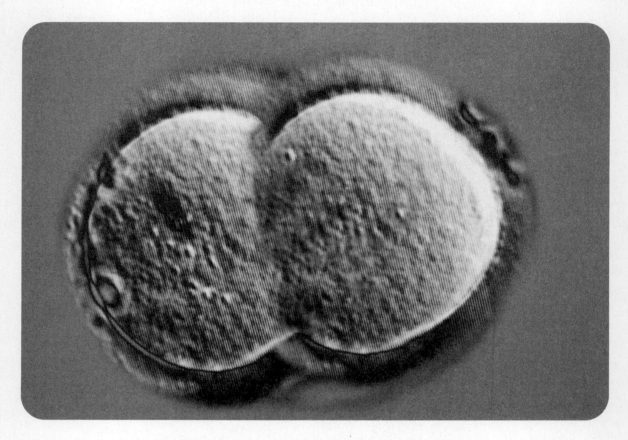

This picture shows a cell dividing into two.

Making New Cells

Every day, billions of human cells die and new cells replace them. Some cells, including some in the nervous system, do not [25] divide. If these cells are damaged, they are not replaced. In these cases, the body may have damage that does not heal. However, in the [50] skin, as well as in other areas of the body, cells die and are replaced all the time. Old skin cells die and new ones [75] are made every 24 hours.

The way in which cells divide to grow and repair themselves is called mitosis. In mitosis, a single cell makes [100] two new cells. When a person's skin is cut, for example, a scab forms. Underneath the scab, skin cells that were not damaged undergo mitosis and replace the damaged cells, healing the cut. [133]

Cells

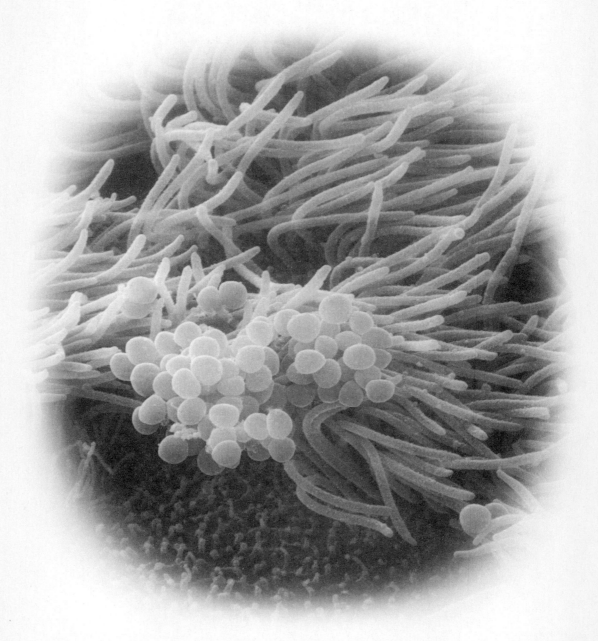

This picture shows staph bacteria as it looks under a microscope.

One-Celled Living Things

Bacteria are living things that have only one single cell. Because bacteria are so small, scientists have to use microscopes to [25] study them. A human body can contain as many as 100 trillion bacteria. Most bacteria are harmless to the body, and some are even helpful. [50] Helpful bacteria break down food and perform other tasks. Harmful bacteria can give off chemical poisons that cause sicknesses, like strep throat, or even tooth [75] decay.

Bacteria can be found in many places on Earth other than in people, animals, or plants. People also use bacteria to perform tasks. For [100] example, some bacteria break down harmful substances in the soil, and some turn milk into cheese. In addition, scientists have found that some forms of bacteria can break up oil spills in oceans. [133]

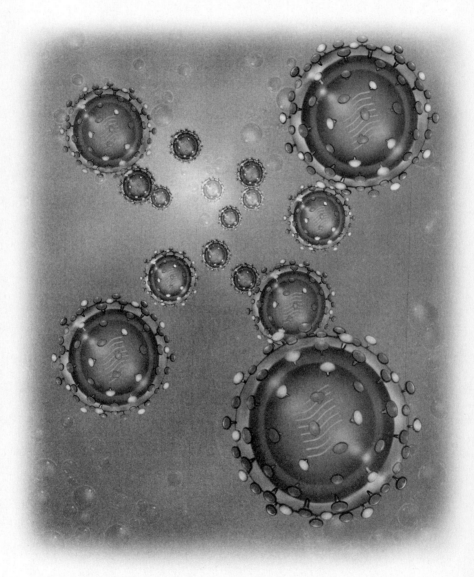

This drawing shows a flu virus as it looks under a microscope.

Cells and Human Disease

Like bacteria, viruses are living things that can cause disease. Viruses are tiny particles that cannot live on their own. Once[25] these particles enter a cell, they increase quickly. When the cell can no longer hold them, it bursts. Then, the disease moves into more cells.[50] Diseases like colds or the flu are caused by viruses increasing and spreading throughout a body's cells.

Another disease that affects cells is called cancer.[75] In cancer, cells divide very quickly, and the new cells form growths called tumors. As a tumor grows, it stops the body from doing its[100] normal work. Some scientists think that this ability of cells to divide quickly can be passed on from parents. Some also think that it can be caused by chemicals, smoking, or lack of exercise.[134]

Write words that will help you remember what you learned.

The Smallest Units of Life

_____

_____

_____

_____

Trillions of Cells

_____

_____

_____

_____

Making New Cells

_____

_____

_____

_____

One-Celled Living Things

_____

_____

_____

_____

Cells and Human Disease

_____

_____

_____

_____

The Smallest Units of Life

1. What is a cell?

    Ⓐ a chloroplast in plants

    Ⓑ a system in the human body

    Ⓒ the smallest unit of living material

    Ⓓ a special type of cork

2. Name two ways plant cells differ from animal cells.

    _____

    _____

    _____

Trillions of Cells

1. What does the human respiratory system do?

    Ⓐ It helps the body breathe.

    Ⓑ It keeps the air passages healthy.

    Ⓒ It makes the heart beat.

    Ⓓ It helps the body digest food.

2. Explain what a system is in the human body.

    _____

    _____

    _____

 **Cells**

Making New Cells

1. What is mitosis?

   Ⓐ the skin cells

   Ⓑ the way cells divide

   Ⓒ how cells are damaged

   Ⓓ the nervous system

2. How does a cut in the skin heal?

   _____

   _____

   _____

One-Celled Living Things

1. What are bacteria?

   Ⓐ living things that are harmful to people

   Ⓑ systems of living things

   Ⓒ living things that have many cells

   Ⓓ living things that have only one cell

2. In what ways can bacteria be both harmful and helpful to people?

   _____

   _____

   _____

Cells and Human Disease

1. This reading is MAINLY about ___

    Ⓐ how disease affects cells.

    Ⓑ how cancer starts.

    Ⓒ viruses that start in cells.

    Ⓓ how colds and the flu spread.

2. How do viruses make people sick?

_____

_____

_____

Connect Your Ideas

1. What are three facts you learned about cells?

_____

_____

_____

2. How do cells work together to keep the human body alive and to make it sick?

_____

_____

_____

The Human Nervous System

When you answer a question, you think about what you know
and make a conscious response.

What Does the Nervous System Do?

Although the body's systems work together, each one has a special job. The nervous system manages the other systems.[25] It collects information on what is happening inside and outside the body and tells the other systems how to respond.

One type of response is[50] a conscious response. People think before making conscious responses, such as answering a question. In a conscious response, the brain considers the information and sends[75] back a message.

Another type of response is an unconscious response. People do not think before making unconscious responses. The beating of the heart is[100] an unconscious response. Reflexes are also unconscious responses. A reflex is triggered when a person jerks away from a flame. In a reflex, the muscles respond *before* the brain gets the information.[132]

The Human Nervous System

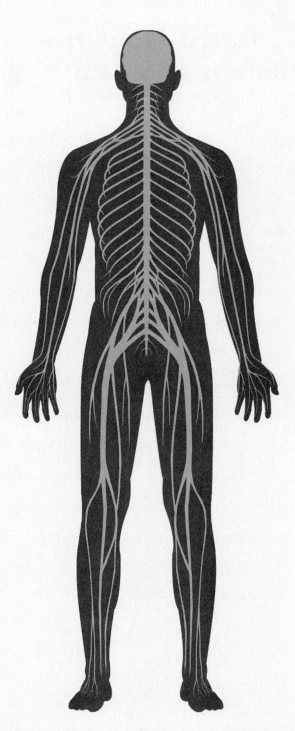

The parts of the nervous system work together to keep the body working and to help people respond to the world.

The Parts of the Nervous System

The nervous system is made up of the brain, the spinal cord, and the nerves. Two of these parts[25] need special protection. The brain, which is the control center of the body, is kept safe by the skull. The spinal cord, which joins the[50] nerves to the brain, is kept safe by the backbones.

The nerves do not have special protection. They are found throughout the body, and their[75] job is to receive information and carry it to the brain. The brain then decides what to do with the information. The nerves also carry[100] information from the brain to the muscles. For example, your nerves tell your brain that a food smells good. Then, your brain tells the nerves in your muscles to eat the food.[132]

The Human Nervous System

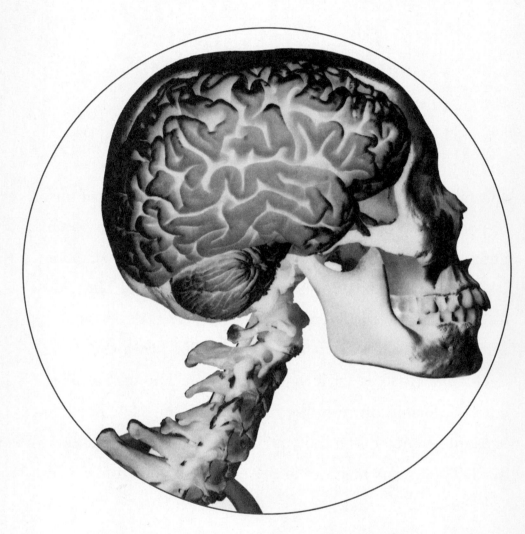

This picture shows how the human skull joins with the backbones.

The Control Center

The human brain, which weighs about three pounds, is not the largest brain on Earth. However, the human brain is the largest[25] when it is compared to the size of the body it is in.

The human brain is also the most complex brain on Earth. It[50] thinks about what is going on around it, and it plans what to do in response. This complex process allows humans to change themselves and[75] the world around them.

The three main parts of the brain are the cerebrum, cerebellum, and brainstem. Thinking and learning take place in the cerebrum.[100] The cerebrum also stores memories. The cerebellum controls muscle movement. The cerebellum also controls balance, keeping the body steady and stable. The brainstem manages basic life jobs, such as breathing and sleeping.[132]

The Human Nervous System

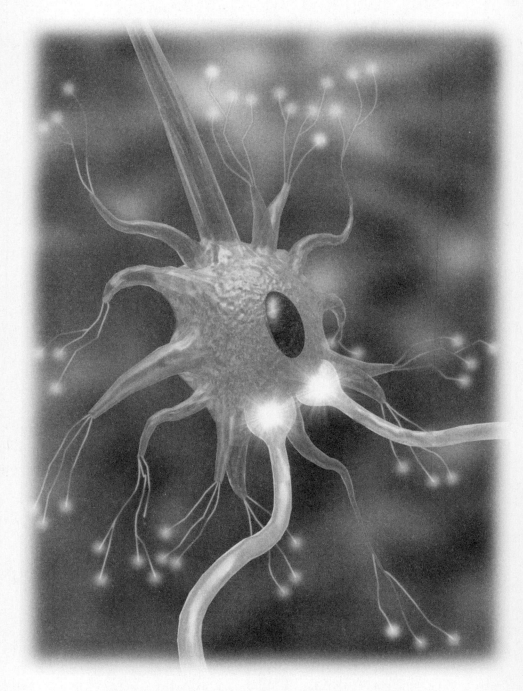

Neurons, like the one shown here, send messages to the muscles of the human body.

Sending Messages

Nerves are made of cells called neurons. There are two kinds of neurons: sensory neurons and motor neurons. Sensory neurons send information from [25] the senses to the brain, telling the brain what is happening. Motor neurons send messages from the brain to the muscles, telling the muscles how [50] to respond to the information.

Neurons are of different sizes and shapes. They can range from a fraction of an inch to about three feet [75] in length. Most neurons look like an insect with thin legs and a long tail.

A neuron's leg-like parts pick up information in the [100] form of electrical signals. These electrical signals travel to the cell's tail, where they jump to the next neuron. Some signals travel very quickly—at about 250 miles per hour. [130]

The Human Nervous System

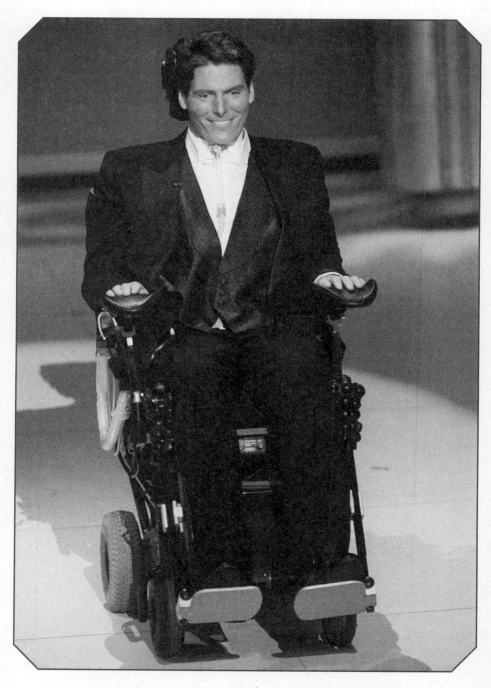

Christopher Reeve's spinal cord was damaged in an accident.
As a result, he could no longer walk.

The Super-Highway

The human spinal cord is made up of a bundle of nerves. It starts at the brain and extends about 18 inches[25] through a hollow in the backbones. The spinal cord is like a super-highway that links the brain and the nerves. Nerves branch off from[50] the spinal cord and go to different parts of the body.

The nerves at the bottom of the spinal cord connect the legs to the[75] brain. If the bottom of the spinal cord is damaged, messages cannot go from the legs to the brain, and people cannot walk.

The nerves[100] at the top of the spinal cord control unconscious tasks, such as breathing. If the top of the spinal cord is damaged, these unconscious tasks can stop, and a person can die.[132]

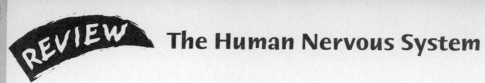

REVIEW **The Human Nervous System**

Write words that will help you remember what you learned.

What Does the Nervous System Do?

_____
_____
_____
_____

The Parts of the Nervous System

_____
_____
_____
_____

The Control Center

_____
_____
_____
_____

Sending Messages

_____
_____
_____
_____

The Super-Highway

_____
_____
_____
_____

What Does the Nervous System Do?

1. Which of the following BEST tells what the nervous system does?

    Ⓐ It makes the heart beat.

    Ⓑ It tells people when to answer questions.

    Ⓒ It manages all of the body's systems.

    Ⓓ It sends messages outside the body.

2. What is the difference between conscious responses and unconscious responses?

    _____

    _____

    _____

The Parts of the Nervous System

1. What do the nerves do?

    Ⓐ protect the spinal cord

    Ⓑ keep the brain safe

    Ⓒ receive and carry information to the brain

    Ⓓ tell the brain what foods are good to eat

2. What are the three parts of the nervous system?

    _____

    _____

    _____

The Control Center

1. Another good name for "The Control Center" is ___

   Ⓐ "The Human Brain."

   Ⓑ "The Cerebrum."

   Ⓒ "The Largest Brain on Earth."

   Ⓓ "Thinking and Learning."

2. What do the three main parts of the brain do?

   _____

   _____

   _____

Sending Messages

1. "Sending Messages" is MAINLY about ___

   Ⓐ how neurons work.

   Ⓑ electrical signals in the brain.

   Ⓒ sending messages to the muscles.

   Ⓓ the leg-like parts of neurons.

2. How do sensory neurons and motor neurons work together?

   _____

   _____

   _____

The Super-Highway

1. What is the spinal cord made of?

Ⓐ the backbones

Ⓑ the brain and the muscles

Ⓒ a bundle of nerves

Ⓓ all of the nerves in the body

2. How is the spinal cord like a super-highway?

_____

_____

_____

Connect Your Ideas

1. Tell three facts you learned about the nervous system.

_____

_____

_____

2. Describe three things your nervous system does every day.

_____

_____

_____

Symbiosis

The small fish near the shark's mouth eats pests that could harm the shark.

What Is Symbiosis?

The word *symbiosis* comes from the Greek words *syn-*, which means "together," and *bios*, which means "life." Scientists use the word *symbiosis* [25] to refer to arrangements in which two kinds of living things, or species, live near each other.

A species of shark and a species of [50] tiny fish show one type of symbiotic arrangement. The fish swim into the shark's mouth and eat pests that can make the shark sick. In [75] return, the shark does not eat the fish. In this way, the fish get food and the shark stays healthy.

Not all symbiotic living arrangements [100] benefit both species. In some cases, symbiotic arrangements harm an animal or plant. A symbiotic arrangement, however, does help at least one species get food, travel from place to place, or stay safe. [133]

Symbiosis

Sea anemones have a symbiotic arrangement with many ocean animals, including the clown fish shown here.

Mutual Benefits

Mutualism is a kind of symbiosis. In this symbiotic living arrangement, both organisms, or living beings, receive mutual benefits.

One example of mutualism [25] is small animals that get their food by cleaning large animals. On the Nile River, in Africa, crocodile birds hop into a crocodile's mouth to [50] eat pests. Crocodiles do not eat crocodile birds. That is because crocodile birds eat the pests that could make crocodiles sick. In return, crocodile birds [75] know where to find food.

Some organisms use symbiotic arrangements for their mutual protection. One species of crab places a sea anemone on its shell. [100] The sea anemone then stings any animal that tries to harm the crab. In exchange, the sea anemone eats the food the crab leaves behind. Both animals benefit from this mutual arrangement. [132]

In this nest, the cuckoo chick is pushing out the eggs of the host bird.

Benefits and Costs

In another kind of symbiotic arrangement, one organism gets food or a safe place to raise its young. This benefit, however, comes [25] at a cost to the other organism. The organism that benefits is called a parasite. The organism that is harmed is called a host.

Parasites, [50] like ticks and fleas, eat by sucking blood from dogs, cats, and other animals. A few parasites may not harm an animal. However, having too [75] many parasites can make an animal sick.

Some parasites also trick a host into caring for the parasite's young. Cuckoos lay their eggs in other [100] birds' nests. Then, when baby cuckoos hatch, they either push their host's eggs out of the nest or kill their host's babies. In this way, cuckoos benefit, but host birds are hurt. [132]

Symbiosis

Spanish moss does not harm trees. Instead, it uses them for support.

Benefits for One

Another kind of symbiotic arrangement is called commensalism. In Latin, *commensalism* means "at the same table." In a commensal living arrangement, although[25] one organism benefits, the other organism is neither hurt nor helped.

The Spanish moss that grows on some oak trees shows commensalism in action. By[50] growing on the high branches of oak trees, Spanish moss gets the sunlight it needs to stay alive. The oak trees on which the Spanish[75] moss grows are neither harmed nor helped by the moss.

An animal that depends on food left behind by another animal also has a commensal[100] living arrangement. Crows that eat the leftovers of a lion's kill benefit by getting a meal without having to hunt. The lion is neither helped nor harmed because he eats first.[131]

Symbiosis

The ants on this bullhorn acacia tree keep the tree free of pests.

Symbiosis in Ants

Some species have different kinds of symbiotic arrangements. Ants, which are divided into about 8,000 species, have symbiotic arrangements with many different[25] kinds of plants and animals. One ant species lives in the bullhorn acacia tree. These ants benefit because they get food and a place to[50] live. The bullhorn acacia tree benefits, too, because the ants keep away animals that might eat its leaves or plants that might grow on it.[75]

However, not all symbiotic arrangements between ants and other species are mutually beneficial. Some ants are parasites. Army ants, for example, can eat any animal[100] they find in their path. Some species of ants even act as parasites to other ants by stealing the host ants' food and by tricking the host ants into raising their young.[132]

Symbiosis

Write words that will help you remember what you learned.

What Is Symbiosis?

_____

_____

_____

_____

Mutual Benefits

_____

_____

_____

_____

Benefits and Costs

_____

_____

_____

_____

Benefits for One

_____

_____

_____

_____

Symbiosis in Ants

_____

_____

_____

_____

What Is Symbiosis?

1. Which of the following BEST describes symbiosis?

   (A) two species that feed together

   (B) two species living near each other

   (C) two species staying safe together

   (D) two species that look alike

2. In this reading, how do the shark and the fish benefit from their symbiotic arrangement?

   _____

   _____

   _____

Mutual Benefits

1. Mutualism is a living arrangement in which ___

   (A) species live together on the Nile River.

   (B) species eat each others' food.

   (C) species stay safe from crocodiles.

   (D) species benefit from living near each other.

2. How do crocodiles and crocodile birds show mutualism?

   _____

   _____

   _____

 **Symbiosis**

Benefits and Costs

1. What is the main idea of "Benefits and Costs"?

   Ⓐ Parasites can make animals sick.

   Ⓑ Host animals benefit from some symbiotic arrangements.

   Ⓒ Some symbiotic arrangements help one organism and hurt another.

   Ⓓ All symbiotic arrangements help both species.

2. Describe a symbiotic arrangement in which one organism is harmed.

   _____

   _____

   _____

Benefits for One

1. Another good name for "Benefits for One" is ___

   Ⓐ "Feeding With Lions."

   Ⓑ "Everyone Benefits."

   Ⓒ "No Help, No Harm."

   Ⓓ "Spanish Moss."

2. What is commensalism?

   _____

   _____

   _____

Symbiosis in Ants

1. "Symbiosis in Ants" is MAINLY about ___

   (A) ants that are parasites.

   (B) different ways ants live with other plants and animals.

   (C) ants that have mutually beneficial arrangements.

   (D) what ants eat and where they live.

2. Describe one example of symbiosis in ants.

_____

_____

_____

Connect Your Ideas

1. Describe two symbiotic arrangements: one in animals and one in plants.

_____

_____

_____

2. Describe one symbiotic arrangement that can help an organism and one that can hurt an organism.

_____

_____

_____

_____

Reading Log • Level F • Book 1

	I Read This	New Words I Learned	New Facts I Learned	What Else I Want to Learn About This Subject
Speeches That Inspire				
The Power of Speech				
The Gettysburg Address				
A Day of Infamy				
A Call to Service				
I Have a Dream				
American Pioneers				
John Muir				
Eleanor Roosevelt				
The Little Rock Nine				
Neil Armstrong				
David Ho				
Celebrating Independence				
Canada Day				
Mexican Independence Day				
Independence Day in the Philippines				
Freedom Day				
Bastille Day				

	I Read This	New Words I Learned	New Facts I Learned	What Else I Want to Learn About This Subject
Cells				
The Smallest Units of Life				
Trillions of Cells				
Making New Cells				
One-Celled Living Things				
Cells and Human Disease				
The Human Nervous System				
What Does the Nervous System Do?				
The Parts of the Nervous System				
The Control Center				
Sending Messages				
The Super-Highway				
Symbiosis				
What Is Symbiosis?				
Mutual Benefits				
Benefits and Costs				
Benefits for One				
Symbiosis in Ants				

Self-Check Graph

Record your reading rate here.

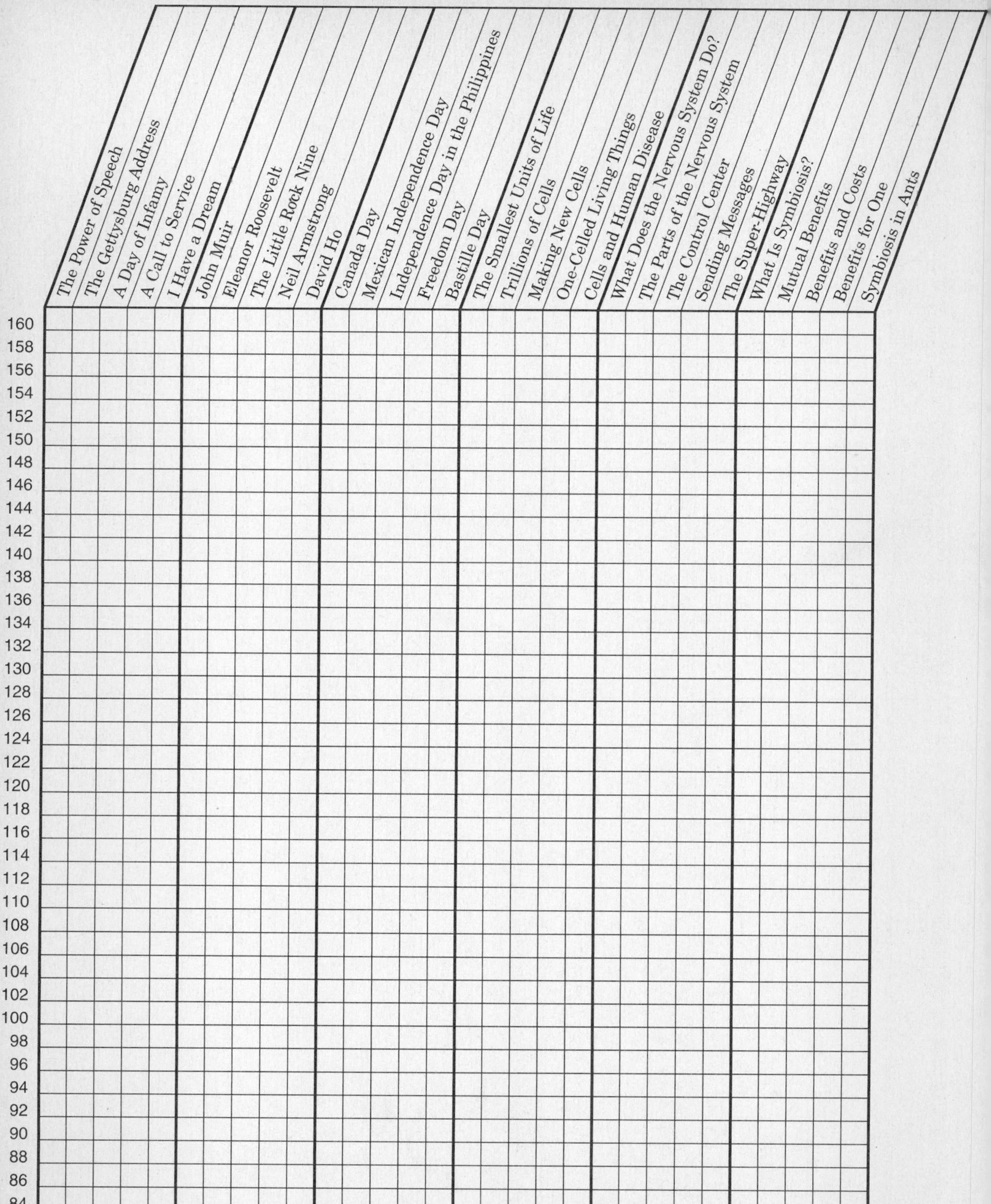
The Power of Speech
The Gettysburg Address
A Day of Infamy
A Call to Service
I Have a Dream
John Muir
Eleanor Roosevelt
The Little Rock Nine
Neil Armstrong
David Ho
Canada Day
Mexican Independence Day
Independence Day in the Philippines
Freedom Day
Bastille Day
The Smallest Units of Life
Trillions of Cells
Making New Cells
One-Celled Living Things
Cells and Human Disease
What Does the Nervous System Do?
The Parts of the Nervous System
The Control Center
Sending Messages
The Super-Highway
What Is Symbiosis?
Mutual Benefits
Benefits and Costs
Benefits for One
Symbiosis in Ants
160
158
156
154
152
150
148
146
144
142
140
138
136
134
132
130
128
126
124
122
120
118
116
114
112
110
108
106
104
102
100
98
96
94
92
90
88
86
84
82
80